SYDNEY HARBOUR

To my dear friend,
wishing you many happy memories
of your time in Sydney and environs,
Much love,
Jill

January 1996

Winter sun on the Opera House – 1992

SYDNEY HARBOUR

David Moore

David Moore

Text by Rodney Hall

CHAPTER & VERSE
in association with
STATE LIBRARY OF NSW PRESS

Ferry terminal, Circular Quay – 1992

First published in 1993 by Chapter & Verse, an imprint of Wellington Lane Press Pty Ltd, 1 King George Street, McMahons Point, NSW 2060 and John Witzig & Company Pty Ltd, Mullumbimby, NSW 2482 in association with the State Library of New South Wales Press.

Reprinted 1994.

Copyright © 1993 Chapter & Verse
Photographs © David Moore unless otherwise acknowledged
Introduction © David Moore
Text © Rodney Hall
Quotation from "Letters to Live Poets – XXXIV" from *Bruce Beaver: New and Selected Poems 1960–1990,* Bruce Beaver, published by University of Queensland Press, 1991.

Printed in Hong Kong by South China Printing Co. Ltd
Typeset by Deblaere Typesetting Pty Ltd, Dee Why, NSW

Designed by John Witzig
Edited by Carol Dettmann

National Library of Australia Cataloguing-in-Publication data:

Moore, David, 1927–
    Sydney Harbour

    ISBN 0 947322 08 6
    ISBN 0 947322 09 4 (pbk.).

    1. Sydney Harbour (N.S.W.) – Pictorial works. I. Hall, Rodney, 1935–
II. Title

994.41

Publication of this book coincided with an exhibition at the State Library of New South Wales in 1993–94, which was generously supported by Hanimex Pty Limited, P&O Australia Ltd and Australian Colour Laboratories Pty Ltd.

Cover: Summer dawn over Sydney from Kirribilli – 1993
Half title: Near Balls Head at dusk – 1962
Back cover: Luna Park entrance – 1982

Pyrmont Bridge and Darling Harbour – 1947

CONTENTS

Orcades departure, Pyrmont – c.1948

FOREWORD

On Sunday 6 May 1770, His Majesty's ship *Endeavour Bark* sailed north from Botany Bay and her Captain, James Cook, noted soon after that his ship was sailing 'about three miles from the land and abreast of a Bay or Harbour wherein there appeared to be safe anchorage'.

Arguably the greatest navigator and discoverer the world has ever known, he was never to learn just what an understatement those words would prove to be.

Some 18 years later, Captain Arthur Philip sailed from Botany Bay with a small contingent in three ship's boats from the First Fleet 'to examine Port Jackson, a bay mentioned by Captain Cook'. The weather conditions on 22 January 1788 were reported by Philip to be 'mild and serene' and one can only imagine the rising excitement that Philip must have felt as he approached and then entered Sydney Harbour for the first time.

Philip was quick to recognise the significance of his discovery:

> We had the satisfaction to find one of the finest harbours in the world, one in which a thousand sail of the line may ride in the most perfect security.

Accounts by other officers of the First Fleet gave more glowing accounts of its beauty. Daniel Southwell, a young naval officer in HMS *Sirius* wrote:

> Nothing can be conceived more picturesque than the appearance of the country while running up the extraordinary harbour. The land on all sides is high and covered with an exuberance of trees and towards the craggy rocks, and wonderful declivities are to be seen everywhere.

The surgeon of HMS *Sirius* wrote that the harbour:

> …exhibited a variety of romantic views, all thrown into sweet confusion by the careless hand of nature.

Those words written so long ago, remain relevant to the Sydney Harbour that we know today.

As a Sydney lad who was privileged to spend much of his adult life at sea, I have had many opportunities to experience Sydney Harbour in all its moods and magnificence. When I was a boy, it provided endless opportunities for adventure – whether exploring its foreshore, fishing from rocky headlands, canoeing and sailing or enjoying the romance of steam on board one's favourite ferry. Later in my life, I sailed into and out of Sydney Harbour on countless occasions in ships of all descriptions and I was always stimulated by each succeeding experience. I never tired of my association with this magnificent waterway.

For Sydney Harbour is truly a jewel in nature's crown; a harbour without equal anywhere in the world. It is the cradle of European settlement in Australia, a repository of our modern history and a place where the creations of man and nature rest easily together.

A harbour of such beauty and stature deserves to be recorded by the best in published art for the benefit of present and future generations. I was therefore delighted to learn that David Moore's photographs of Sydney Harbour, spanning a period of almost 50 years, were to be brought together in book form. For David's artistry and skill as a photographer are renowned. His portrayal of a harbour which he has known for much of his life will surely be a labour of love which will delight all who have experienced the majesty of Sydney Harbour.

His Excellency Rear Admiral Peter Sinclair, AC
Governor of New South Wales

INTRODUCTION

David Moore

To grow up within a kilometre or two of Sydney Harbour is a particular privilege. All children need playgrounds: for me the harbour waters and foreshores existed as a world of delight, adventure and mystery. This waterway was an extension of my being from the age of ten or eleven.

Bushland reserves with sunlight bouncing off the water's surface provided an environment that was ideal for playing 'goodies and baddies'. With my brother Tony, Don from across the road and Wal from next door, we spent tense, excited hours stalking each other past rock cliffs, pink angophoras and banksias. Our weapons were homemade catapults of forked sticks and inner tube rubber. We gathered ammunition from pittosporum trees that grew hard, yellow berries, for stones were sensibly banned as missiles.

Along the shoreline rocks and beaches we found strange flotsam, and used our fishing tackle to catch yellowtail, sweep and sometimes line-tangling eels from the rock crevices. Once I saw a 1.5m carpet shark cruising through the clear water just a step from where I was perched. Occasionally we would wade the beach shallows at night with kerosene lantern and scoop nets to catch prawns and witness a multitude of nocturnal creatures.

My one-boy canoe, made at school from split cane and canvas, allowed dangerous freedom from the water's edge. With growing confidence in my ability to remain upright, I successfully completed voyages far from shore.

Unfortunately, my rudimentary box camera was not carried on these excursions; but I did take it to Watsons Bay to record big game fish hanging on the scale, and also sometimes on ferry rides. Years later I used my Rolleicord to photograph children on the foreshores doing what I had done as a child.

The night of 31 May 1942 seemed unremarkable as I prepared for sleep on the balcony of our Vaucluse house which my architect/painter father had designed and built in 1927. The war in the Pacific, far to the north of Sydney, was not providing politicians in Canberra – or Washington – reason for optimism. Milne Bay in New Guinea was about to fall to the advancing Japanese and the Kokoda Trail – that hellish mudslide – was in danger of being overrun. The future for a secure Australia looked as black as the Sydney night.

At about midnight I suddenly flicked wide awake as explosions and gunfire echoed around the harbour residential suburbs. Looking to the west, I saw searchlights scanning the water near Garden Island and fiery tracer shells in near horizontal trajectories. There was a confusion apparent suggesting that something really important, and directly related to the distant conflict, was taking place as I watched.

An ancient telescope set up on the balcony enabled me to witness the action in relatively close detail. It was obvious that Sydney Harbour was suddenly and awesomely a new theatre of the war. Our lurking fears were justified: the Japanese were here.

As daylight smudged the north shore hills into form there was activity in Taylor Bay, directly across the harbour from our house. A naval craft sped across the water. In its wake a crown of white rose from the surface, followed by a delayed, muffled *thrump*. A depth charge. It was only then that the possibility of a submarine raid within the harbour seemed real.

The events of that night, so traumatic for Sydney, proved the closest I have ever come to armed conflict. Although indelibly etched in my memory, it is perhaps regretful that my little box camera was not used to document the drama. Partly this was due to my being transfixed by the event; partly, I realise in retrospect, the standard focal length lens coupled with my lack of photographic knowledge would have registered little of value. Yet I wish I had taken just one exposure as an experiment.

When my photographic ability had increased, I took documentary pictures of the maritime areas of Pyrmont and Darling Harbour with freighters, tugs and work boats polluting the air with coal-fired engines. The low-rise city formed a theatrical, often mist-softened backdrop to the activity on the water with the engineering geometry of structures such as Pyrmont Bridge sometimes strong in the foreground.

The departure of ocean liners was always climactic. A carnival feeling was in the air with well-wishers, thousands of coloured paper streamers and a general air of excitement as the ships gave three deep-throated blasts before moving astern to begin the long voyage to the United Kingdom.

In 1951 I sailed from Sydney aboard the pristine new liner *Oronsay* bound for seven years of work and travel overseas. Further photographic exploration of the harbour and city would have to wait for my eventual return.

I was on deck at dawn in 1958 when the return voyage to Australia neared an end. With the proud cliff of North Head to starboard the ship left the open sea and quietly entered harbour waters. Tugs sidled alongside as the city, illuminated by the rising sun, came into view. All was reflected in the mirror surface and the ship's mast seemed to scrape the great steel span of the Harbour Bridge as we headed for the same Pyrmont dock from which my father had farewelled me seven years before. I was transfixed by the spectacle. Today, arrival in Australia through an anonymous air terminal cannot compare with the theatrical experience of a shipboard homecoming.

Once the pleasant turmoil of returning had subsided it was not long before I again yielded to the beckoning desire to photograph the city and its complex waterway. Much had changed in my absence with economic forces of development increasing the value of harbour-front real estate. The central business district witnessed the growing steel frame of Sydney's first truly highrise corporate headquarters in the AMP building at Circular Quay. Home unit slabs rose on prime foreshores causing Council legislation to be amended to prevent a wall of private development obscuring the view from properties behind. After years of indecision, excavation work began on the magnificent concept of the Sydney Opera House.

There was much to record, and my photojournalism experience overseas provided an added awareness that replaced the naïve joy of previous years. Quite suddenly, I realised it was possible to make valid statements about my country that might add to our concept of national identity.

I accepted assignments from major international magazines with enthusiasm and boundless energy. *Time-Life Books* provided scope for harbour pictures with a commission to photograph Australia and New Zealand. So too did the *National Geographic Magazine* as part of a coverage of New South Wales. But the most pertinent assignment, relative to Sydney, came from *Life Magazine* when bitter division of opinion forced the resignation of Joern Utzon – architect of the

Opera House. His visionary structure was rising on Bennelong Point when the New South Wales Minister for Public Works, Davis Hughes, used an iron fist to enforce his will. I was an observer of the conflict.

Invited to the site by Government Architect Edward Farmer to give his opinion on the colour of the precast cladding on the podium walls, Hughes stood close to the erected test panels, poked the surface, then turned to me to enquire 'which do you prefer?'. I was appalled that such an important decision could be placed in the hands of the Minister for Public Works (much less a visiting photographer) and politely registered my attitude. There followed a brief portrait session in which I attempted to portray Davis Hughes as the villain in this tragic scenario.

A tide of assisted-passage migrants arrived regularly at the Sydney Cove Passenger Terminal. While on assignment for the *National Geographic,* I rose early to photograph the liner *Galileo Galilei* rounding Bennelong Point and approaching the dock. Observing the passenger decks I noticed a group of migrants spanning four generations searching for familiar faces in the welcoming crowd. As I closed in with a 200mm lens every face expressed varying emotions. Suddenly the woman in the middle of the group gestured to acknowledge a dockside greeting and my picture came together. Originally exposed in colour, I later converted it to black and white, which I prefer. Somehow colour becomes a barrier in the reading of emotional expression.

When considering the parameters of this book and the exhibition at the State Library of New South Wales, I wished to echo the feeling of standing on the deck of a great ocean liner at sunrise while entering the harbour. Because the surrounding hills of the waterway exist as protecting arms, I thought about the possibility of a 360 degree panorama in 14 sections to express the idea. With its mid-harbour position, the island of Fort Denison seemed to be the ideal location. But what problems would have to be overcome to produce a successful image? Considered in detail they were daunting.

The top of the martello tower at Fort Denison was selected as the vantage point, however a central lighthouse precluded the possibility of a single camera position. The answer lay in deciding on an easterly *and* a westerly tripod position, so each would provide a 180 degree sweep. I was concerned about the sky, because moving clouds in a sectional panorama could be distracting on the picture abutments. There was no way they would join successfully. Clear sky conditions were essential.

Since I wanted to have the light of the sunrise illuminating the city, shooting towards the east required fighting direct sun in the camera lens – an awesome technical problem. But lateral thinking and a certain logic came to the rescue. I reasoned that if the eastern sky segments were exposed *before* sunrise, the sun would rise as the camera angles moved towards north and south with the western segments finally being shot with direct sun illumination. Not only would this be a workable technical solution, but it would also impart a time factor into the final result. The viewer would then experience pre-sunrise as well as post-sunrise light within the one composite image. The idea was intriguing.

However my pre-planning did not allow for errors of judgement; if an insoluble problem arose, the exercise could have been a total failure. I was a tense bundle of nerves for a day before the shoot until the last frame was exposed. Success balanced on a fine edge of hope. My relief when viewing the processed film was profound and I hope the results convey a measure of the glory of Sydney Harbour on a sublime winter morning in August 1992.

Today, whenever I see diamond points of sunlight dancing on the surface of the harbour waters, I feel a dimly-remembered chord of nostalgia. Although I have tried to isolate the connection many times, it remains elusive. Certainly it is to do with the *quality* of Sydney light, which seems unique in the world, but more particularly it may relate to my childhood experience among the angophoras and rocks of harbourside reserves.

The collection of pictures in this book is a personal response to an environment that never ceases to beguile, however in no sense can one photographer's observation ever be definitive. Others will come and see it with fresh eyes. My statement seeks to pay homage to a gift of rare beauty.

Double exposure SS *Morinda*
Yacht at Watsons Bay
Mako shark, Watsons Bay – all c.1940

Sunrise at Man O' War Steps – c.1947

Tug at Pyrmont – c.1947

Rose Bay flying boat base in winter fog – c.1948

Woolloomooloo Bay and Garden Island in winter fog – c.1948

Boys at play on waterfront – c.1947

Pile-driver at Pyrmont – c.1947

Dockworkers and *Titan* crane – c.1947

Titan, floating crane, Darling Harbour – c.1947

Port Brisbane, Pyrmont – c.1947
Timber wharf at Rozelle Bay – c.1947

Port Chalmers, *Orontes* and *Port Brisbane*, Pyrmont docks – c.1947

Mast of HMAS *Sydney*, Bradleys Head – c.1948

Manly ferry *Dee Why* and lighthouse, Bradleys Head – c.1947

Vaucluse waterfront – c.1947

Fishing trawler and freighter in morning light – c.1948

Rigging 18 footer, Rose Bay – c.1948
18 footer and Shark Island lighthouse – c.1948

Afternoon light and 18 footer – c.1948

Balmain waterfront – c.1947

Erskine Street wharf and Balmain ferry – c.1947

Boy on ferry, Darling Harbour – c.1947

Erskine Street and AWA radio tower – c.1947

Sydney Harbour Bridge 2 – 1947

Pyrmont Bridge and the city – 1947

Darling Street, Balmain – c.1947

Darling Harbour and Pyrmont docks – c.1948

The city and Fort Denison from bridge of *Himalaya* – 1950

Well-wishers and streamers, Pyrmont – c.1948

Departure of *Orcades*, Pyrmont – c.1948

Orcades and well-wishers, Pyrmont – c.1948

Orcades and afternoon light – 1949

THE PORT

Deeply implanted in the human mind is the notion of the haven. So universal is its appeal we apply it to the pressures of love, war, and life itself. As always with popular images of this kind the profound truth embedded there can be revived at a touch of the actual. Sydney Harbour is the ultimate haven. We recognise this instantly. We don't have to be persuaded or shown statistical evidence. The peace of this magnificent expanse of water answers a need within us.

Fifty years ago, when David Moore took his first photographs here, the harbour was the working heart of Sydney. The city still retained its character as a seafaring centre. Travellers constantly sailed out on long voyages. Others sailed in. A vast and shifting volume of freight was forever being unloaded from dozens of ships of all sizes and nationalities; just as a vast and shifting volume was forever being loaded on to them.

This was the era of the port.

Cargo ships were the lifeblood of the nation's trade. Passenger liners brought immigrants in and took tourists away to Britain and other European destinations. Small craft swarmed around the waterways delivering individual services, providing pleasure, or pushing and pulling the great vessels. Cranes and crates crowded docks busy with labourers.

The first transformations of the harbour two hundred years ago were precisely for this: to develop it as a port.

In 1788 those eleven ships comprising the First Fleet sailed into a world their occupants had never encountered before – a very particular wilderness in which people had lived since long before the waters of the last melting Ice Age flooded in to drown their old tribal grounds, creating a seashore among what were once mountainous gullies and a harbour from a river course – a wilderness unmarked by such imperatives as 'property', which lay at the heart of the invading culture. To those British eyes the wooded shores may even have seemed so unshaped and uncultivated as to be a kind of chaos. So they came in: wooden ships gliding on the smooth water of this breathtaking haven, bringing a cargo of ideas that would change the place forever.

Thickets and swamps were cleared and drained to make room for tiny outposts which began dotting the coves. The typical settlement consisted of a wharf with one or two sheds on the shore, a track winding up among dense trees to the top of the ridge where more clearing was taking place for a hamlet to cluster round a handsome house – built by some gentleman settler on the profits of convict labour and his subsequent trade in merchandise of one kind or another – very much the British model. These houses may still be found, embedded in the clutter of suburbia.

The new rich took their pick. There was a seemingly inexhaustible choice of building sites offering vistas of vast skies, rocky foreshores and hills beyond, blossoming wattles among angophora forest, and the water – such a fabulous spread of water – in all its mercurial moods. Windmills stood squeaking on the rises and church towers emerged among shingle roofs and grey slate roofs.

Just as the rivers were being used as the main routes inland so the expanse of harbour became a connecting link with a web of regular ferries visiting the little wharves.

More blocks of forest were cleared and gardens laid out. Here and there at strategic points the colonial authorities built walled gun batteries and furnished them with cannon, stationing troopers there to prevent any invasion by rival marauding Europeans. The little island of Pinchgut, prominent in the middle of the harbour, was completely enveloped in fortifications and surmounted by a martello tower.

The harbour, secured for the empire at the huge cost of the convict system, was indeed a priceless asset. Ever since the first ships carrying whale and seal oil set out through the Heads, bound for India, the true nature of Sydney as a trading post was confirmed.

But as the settlement expanded things changed. The flocks of parrots so often remarked alighting among the trees of the town grew less and less common, the kangaroos were shot or driven away, roads snaked round the points and the ridgetop hamlets spread down to the water's edge. Picnic spots were cleared and regularly used. Scenic paths were laid out. Other areas of foreshore lay barren and dusty while bullocks dragged shattered tree trunks around and workmen with adzes sweated at the essential job of building fences: essential because fencing represented the archetypal European notion of what to do with land. Land must be divided up. Animals must be kept in and people kept out. The concept of ownership transformed the harbour which had never before been carved up into petty territories. Industry was established. Sawmills at the water's edge spouted endless plumes of smoke from their tall stacks. The noise must have seemed unbearably harsh, clanking and echoing over the quiet waters.

Despite this, the machinery was very small scale. The British brought with them an eighteenth century culture, a conservatism that renounced the squalor of the Industrial Revolution taking over their own country. Here in the colonies, so they thought, free settlers could rediscover an Arcadian simplicity. And even the debased convicts might hopefully be restored as useful members of society with some chance of a decent life ahead of them. The bitter truth was that the convicts had already been useful indeed, as free labour – slave labour – for just about every building project during the founding of the city, besides their use as free labour on farms as well.

The irony was extraordinary. From the settler's point of view there was seen to be something gentlemanly about the challenge of leaving England and tackling the heroic task of carving another England from a landscape wholly foreign to any such design. Similarly from the point of view of the Irish political prisoners, as England's enemies, the new town would one day offer hope, a fresh beginning, a place where men and women might speak out and be free from the worst oppression by authority. In a sense, they were both right. The secret lay not just in the open spaces they found here and the availability of limitless land but in the nature of the new society they established.

The old order had already been thrown into confusion by industry: its clearly defined hierarchy of aristocrats, gentry, clergy, military and peasants had been rocked to the foundations by a proliferation of factories, by the spawning of huge urban centres cut off from contact with the countryside or the old graces of seigneurial obligations, by the rise of a new class of wealthy manufacturers and by the cataclysm of a mobile workforce that suddenly downed tools in the fields and flocked to the big towns.

In Australia adherents to the old order felt they could stem this tide. And the so-called Bunyip Aristocracy took its role very seriously. The paradox was that the orderliness of this newly created society had so little in common with that of a squire with his willing vassals that it needed to be enforced by a militia: so the new Arcadia was compromised from the outset. Nevertheless society in New South Wales did retain some of the pastoral values which were fast being lost in the scramble for unregulated profits in England.

Thanks to a massive army, the British Empire was the world's largest free trade area at the time. This was the main reason for Scotland's decision to enter the Union in 1707, with access to the colonial trade offering such huge opportunities. And, at the other end of the equation, the colonists knew this. Adventurers who came to Australia and New Zealand (including a great many Scots) did so in the conviction that they could enjoy the best of two worlds: the old values of a landed gentry imposing rural stability, plus the prospect of unbridled commercial wealth in the future. At the root of their optimism was an ingrained belief that just as the origins of England's wealth during the Middle Ages had been wool, so it might be here. Wool was accepted as the best prospect for long-term development.

Of all the ships calling into the port at Sydney the most glamorous were the wool clippers. These magnificent four-masters raced one another across vast tracts of ocean and, by navigating the trade winds, they could outstrip the new steam ships. *Thermopylae* held the record, completing the journey from London in sixty days.

By and large the hopes of the optimists, immigrants and ex-convicts, were realised. At great cost of human life and effort, at great cost to the long-term fertility of the land, and at great cost to the original inhabitants, the Arcadian dream was forged into a reality. And the Australian colonies flourished so vigorously they began to agitate for national independence.

Within a hundred years Sydney became a substantial city. By night the glossy black waters were made brilliant and glamorous by the passage of lighted steamers. Big ships berthed at Circular Quay. Paved streets were lined with fine public buildings. The city settled into its shape and character as a place to live and work in.

In 1943 the young David Moore began to capture this character in his early photographs. The harbour as he saw it then was very much as I myself found it six years later when I first sailed in as a boy of thirteen. We came on a ship full of British migrants. The war still loomed huge in our memories. Right through the bombing and the threat of a German invasion the promise of a family return to Australia had represented freedom from the terror. At last it had come true. After six weeks of exciting discomfort at sea – the boredom of confinement aboard occasionally interrupted by the dazzling surprise of such foreign places as Aden and Colombo – the SS *Ranchi* approached Sydney Heads.

It was a dull August morning. I had never thought Sydney could have cold weather. We were up at dawn and I remember feeling cross and difficult. All nine hundred passengers (by now hateful to the last person) crowded on to the decks ahead of us. My sister and I were obliged to wriggle among them to secure places at the rail. I carried a copy of *The Young Traveller in Australia* which a family friend had given us.

We had taken turns reading this book on the way to Port Said, then through the Suez Canal (with a camel train plodding along beside us, seen above the bank of sand as bridled heads and swaying loaded humps) and had finished it in the stifling glaze of light while our ship went gliding through the oily waters of the Red Sea. The author promised us a life of prosperity in Australia, a life of fun in the open air. So we knew this was our due. The book became a talisman, especially during rough weather crossing the Great Australian Bight. As the young traveller in person, I do not recall whether or not the author invited me to picture the land as having been already inhabited by peoples who were dispossessed, or explained that the price of an enviable lifestyle had been paid in human misery and exploitation.

Then at last we found ourselves arriving. My job, cross though I was, consisted of determinedly ignoring the dullness of the day. We rolled and pitched as we turned side-on to the swell. The sea hissed past and the ship's engines thundered. The gap between the Heads opened out. We headed in.

The thudding of the great engines cut back to a quiet pulse. We slid through grey silky waters. A magical world enveloped us. I remember nothing else of the harbour except that we were suddenly docking and I had to be woken out of a trance and dragged away from the section of rail which needed to be removed as part of the mooring process. I had been lost to myself while the great haven was printed on my soul. And now there we were, at a huge ugly timber wharf, the journey over. My sister scolded me because without knowing it I had apparently let *The Young Traveller in Australia* slip from my hand and fall in the water.

THE NEW HOME

Tens of thousands of migrants arrived each year to make a new life for themselves. Contrary to common assumptions, Australia at the end of the forties was not a simple xenophobic Anglo-Celtic outpost. Ever since the gold rushes of last century people of many nationalities had come and stayed: Chinese and Germans wherever gold was found, White Russian refugees in Brisbane, Greeks and Yugoslavs venturing into all manner of remote corners, and Italians pioneering fruit growing districts. These and many more. What was new immediately after World War II was the sheer weight of numbers.

Undoubtedly these new arrivals were met with suspicion and prejudice in many cases, but no more than was the case anywhere else in the world during this tremendous diaspora. Here at least they were for the most part welcomed into the system as 'New Australians' rather than being encouraged to live separately in ghetto-like enclaves. The proverbial generosity of the locals made their reception at least tolerable. Where serious outbursts of racism broke out against Europeans it was generally a reaction against the *scale* of migration. An important factor was the cost to the nation of subsidising these £10 passages, especially with memories of mass unemployment during the Great Depression still very much alive.

The long voyage from the other side of the world involved crossing some pretty wild seas. For the most part people slept in crowded dormitory cabins for twelve or fourteen, families being split up by sexes. Even when they landed, sunburned and bearing bizarre souvenirs from Arabia and Ceylon, they faced the prospect of temporary accommodation in migrant camps with rudimentary facilities. Yet they came. Thousands upon thousands of them. And after the long journey they faced this arrival as a tremendous climax of hope and anxiety.

Himalaya entering Sydney Harbour at dawn – 1950

Himalaya and Fort Denison – 1950

Himalaya approaching Pyrmont docks – 1950

Slinging passengers' baggage – 1950

Customs inspection of passengers' baggage – 1950

Himalaya at night, Pyrmont – 1950

Superstructure design – 1950

Off-loading cargo – 1950

Imported British cars on Pyrmont dock – 1950

Galley of *Himalaya*
Ship's laundry

Seamen cleaning the funnel
Lascar seamen holystoning the deck – all 1950

Painting the *Himalaya* – 1950

Unloading tea from Ceylon – 1950
Loading provisions on Pyrmont dock – 1950

Refrigerated cargo stowage – 1950

First class cabin party before departure – 1950

Departure of the *Himalaya*, Pyrmont – 1950

Himalaya passing Bennelong Point – 1950

THE BRIDGE

The city was firmly established on the south side of the harbour but by the 1840s there was also a smaller second town facing it across the water.

Unless these North Shore residents cared to travel by road out through Parramatta at the far western end of the harbour, they had to commute by boat. The idea of a bridge across the main harbour was suggested in 1857 but the project was shelved as too big. Then in the 1880s the completion of two lesser bridges – the Gladesville Bridge over the Parramatta River and the Fig Tree Bridge over the Lane Cove River – shortened the road journey by 20 kilometres.

Sydney was no longer simply a port, with wharves and warehouses, stores and chandleries ringed by hotels, nor was it simply a garrison town guarding the port.

The city already enveloped the harbour and spread inland to the foot of the mountains. The inhabitants were no longer itinerant visitors or lags serving out their time. They were settled. But once the villages around the waterway were linked together as a single entity the problem of better access from one to another grew acute, especially for freight and carriages.

A rapidly multiplying population crowded the ferries each day until by 1890 wharf queues were established as a notorious joke, with the Sydney Harbour Ferry Company at full stretch carrying 65 million foot passengers during that one year, plus 379,000 horse-drawn vehicles and 45,000 horses with riders.

In 1885 the idea of twin tunnels under the harbour had been put forward as a solution: one tunnel for the railway and the other for a road. Bearing in mind the coalmines already dug at Cremorne and in the Hunter River valley, such tunnels were quite within the reach of Sydney engineers at the time. And so, perhaps, was the big bridge. But neither project found sufficient backing or sufficient government enthusiasm even though a Royal Commission had enquired into the matter and compared eight schemes for bridges, for tunnels, and for combinations of both.

Then came the automobile. Everything changed. The family car achieved instant and overwhelming popularity. Roads had to be improved. And the urge for the two sides of the divided town to reach out across the water to one another became irresistible.

Although nothing had come of the enquiry everyone knew that a solution had to be found.

The right man emerged at the right moment. In 1913 Dr J.J.C. Bradfield, an engineer with the Department of Works, added his voice to the call for a bridge, and caught the public imagination with his plan for a daring single-span cantilever structure. Not only this, but he had thought of a way to fund it – he argued that lots of extra money would come from increased tax revenue on improved land values at the approaches to both ends of the bridge. Just as Bradfield attracted enthusiastic supporters he also stirred up some vociferous opponents: precisely the right recipe for getting something done. Then, as fate would have it, war broke out. Further action on the matter was held over. But during the Great War he used his time to refine and develop the idea, switching from a cantilever to a single arch bridge. Finally in 1923 (more than thirty years after the commission of enquiry had brought down its recommendations), tenders were called. Construction began that same year with the turning of the first sod.

Sydney Harbour Bridge rose simultaneously from either bank, like a slow-motion drama, and met far above the water: so lofty that it dominated the inner harbour, with its high-slung road and railway allowing adequate clearance for the largest ocean liners to pass underneath.

The bridge was opened on 19 March 1932.

The planned ceremony, which began as a dull enough affair, developed into a typically Sydney-style spectacular. Everything had been rather low key and routine, apart from an Aboriginal gumleaf band, men from Wallaga Lake Mission dressed in loin cloths, producing patriotic tunes at piercing volume. Then the unexpected happened. Just as the State Premier made ready to snip the ribbon with his official silver scissors a horsemen broke from the crowd to canter across the wide bare roadway. He wielded a sabre. This was Francis Edward de Groot, self-styled Colonel of the New Guard (a right wing chauvinist organisation which provided D.H. Lawrence with the idea for his novel *Kangaroo*). He slashed the ribbon, stealing the show from right under the noses of the establishment.

The official party's horror gave Sydneysiders enormous satisfaction. Never mind De Groot's questionable politics, never mind the fact that people were suffering terrible hardships at the depths of the Great Depression: an impudent loner on horseback stealing the limelight at a state occasion struck exactly the right chord in a country whose only two folk heroes, Ned Kelly and Ben Hall, were both bushrangers.

The north and south shores were drawn closer together and the sense of a close-knit city enormously strengthened.

The bridge was immediately crowded with motor vehicles and stayed that way.

Sydney was no longer just a port but a city serving its hinterland and spreading far to the west, north and south, spilling out along a hundred kilometres of beaches and spawning strings of satellite towns fanning out like a broken spider's web – towns soon to be linked and merged as mere suburbs of the whole. And yet in the process Sydney never lost the special character given it by the harbour, or the sense of surprise created by so many little coves and inlets reaching in among these suburbs. A common Sydney experience is to come to the crest of a hill and find the street ends in a calm sheet of water. The saw-toothed terrace housing is as inseparable from this hilliness as the hilliness is from the way the original roads so often led to wharves or overgrown bridlepaths or strips of parkland looping the water's edge.

These streets are still there, often with a pub on the corner where drinkers in the saloon bar chalk their cues at a pool table or, in the newly gentrified suburbs, where diners clink glasses under sun umbrellas glimpsed through an old coachway.

While keeping its quirky character a new glittering crowdedness and a change of scale happened as the early landmarks dwindled in among Mondrian effects of checkered tower blocks. There have been basically two cities on the same site: the old city of brick and stone and the new city of steel and concrete.

Yet even while the skyline changed and clumps of multistorey buildings took over, the connections with the port remained, though less dominant in the city's affairs. Those great migrant ships, sailing in from war-ruined Europe, unloaded a work force of labourers to accelerate the change.

Waves of them arrived during the 1950s. Many travelled inland to work on the massive Snowy River hydro-electric scheme and stayed when it was finished, drifting back to the city. A high percentage of construction workers erecting the new central business district were migrants. Some building sites were known to be Italian-speaking jobs, or Serbo-Croat speaking jobs.

A new ferment had set the whole of Australian society fizzing, and nowhere more than Sydney. Migrants in such numbers challenged our sense of belonging, invading the place (much as the British had invaded before them), bringing foreign values and expectations, introducing new foods and new styles. But above all they challenged the simple exclusiveness of us and them and complicated our notions of what was acceptable in behaviour and appearance and what was not – even to modifying ideas of right and wrong. Of course there was a vigorous rearguard reaction against them. But the result was inevitable.

An essential element of that migrant experience is captured here in the suite of three photographs of a black-clad woman arriving – showing her transformation from a sibylline figure straight out of Greek tragedy filled with timeless and unrelenting stoicism, her disillusion being broken apart to open out as vulnerable joy, until she finally surrenders to relief: a relief made deeply moving by the original guardedness which had told so much about her previous life.

In common with others of her kind, she doubtless soon found that the hope and expectation themselves would need to stand the ancient test of dreams going sour, as life bogged down in routine for so many who had expected so much. On the other hand, there was something special to be found here, perhaps particularly in those days. The newcomers eagerly grasped at an opportunity to earn incomes that gave them a wholly new independence. To look at the range of faces lining the rail of an arriving ship was to see the play of anxieties and hopes in hundreds of expressions, from the eager to the apprehensive to the imperiously bored.

In a book of photographs such as this, one of the most fascinating aspects is the lapse of time combined with the silence of photographed images. We turn the pages and watch the city transmogrifying itself, regenerating, miraculously throwing up new features like an independent form of life. And, as part of the change, even the focal point of the city shifts, first from the docks to the railway station and then to an area around Town Hall midway between them while an ugly freeway straddles Circular Quay and the waterfront seems to a great measure bypassed.

Then came an extraordinary event, extraordinary enough to transfigure the great harbour itself. Fort Macquarie, built in 1821, which had been modified later and converted into a giant tram shed, was pulled down. The squared battlemented walls were reduced to a heap of rubble. Bennelong Point, the key site of the harbour (and the only one named for an Aboriginal inhabitant), was being cleared ready for a controversial new structure.

The Sydney Opera House is the result of the visionary ideas of two men: Sir Eugene Goossens who was then conductor of the Sydney Symphony Orchestra, and Joern Utzon, architect. Goossens promoted the original suggestion for a performing arts complex and he was the one who advocated the Bennelong Point site. He already had a high profile, having successfully created a fine ensemble from the rudimentary Sydney Symphony Orchestra he found here when he arrived from Britain. Yet he was destined to be hounded out of Australia for having concealed in his baggage an assortment of pornographic publications and sex-aid objects which, within a few years, would be readily available in most major cities.

The link between the two men had begun when the New South Wales state Labor Government of the day announced a worldwide competition for an opera house design for the site and appointed a distinguished panel of judges. The judges (all but one) sat for eleven days studying 222 entries. They had already selected a short list of ten when the famous

Finnish-American architect Eero Saarinen, the last of the panel to arrive, rejected the lot as not interesting enough. He asked to see the rejects and seized on the design by Joern Utzon. He insisted on having this entry reinstated and included in the shortlist. Then with great energy he set about the task of persuading the others that this had to be the winner.

The nation is in his debt that he succeeded. The result was the only great building in the country; and one of the few great buildings of the 1960s. Troubled as its history was, scandalously as the great architect was treated, though it divided the community and though one faction behaved with such extraordinary spitefulness and narrow mindedness that the names of Premier Robin Askin and his Minister for Public Works, Mr Davis Hughes, are now synonymous with a brutish hangover from our unsophisticated past, the Opera House was built. It rose on its peerless site like an opening flower, a miraculously daring concept perfectly in tune with the new emergent spirit of Sydney, to become not only the quintessential symbol of the city (superseding the bridge) but a symbol for the whole nation.

Sydney Cove and Bennelong Point – 1958

Manly ferry and Unilever building, Circular Quay – 1958

Manly ferry *North Head* with city backdrop – 1976

Ferry *Evelyn Star* and liner, Circular Quay – 1961

Ferry commuters – 1963

Ferry *North Head* and boys fishing, Circular Quay – 1976

Morning peak traffic on Harbour Bridge – 1959

The Rocks district from Harrington Street – 1960

Gladesville Bridge – 1965
Pyrmont Bridge – 1962

Southern approach to Harbour Bridge – 1964

Cahill Expressway at Circular Quay – 1962

Cahill Expressway and Circular Quay traffic – 1963

Sydney Harbour after sunrise looking east – 1963

Sydney Harbour from 16,000 feet – 1966

Start of Sydney to Hobart yacht race – 1963

Wind patterns on harbour waters – 1967

Tug deckhand and mooring buoy – 1963

Oriana entering Sydney Harbour – 1963

Migrant aboard *Galileo Galilei* – 1966

Migrants arriving in Sydney – 1966

Oriana berthing at Sydney Cove Passenger Terminal – 1963

Ship maintenance, Balmain – 1960

Dockworker and cask, Circular Quay – 1963

Ship painters, Circular Quay – 1961

8 am traffic on Harbour Bridge – 1985

Harbour Bridge from west Rocks – 1978

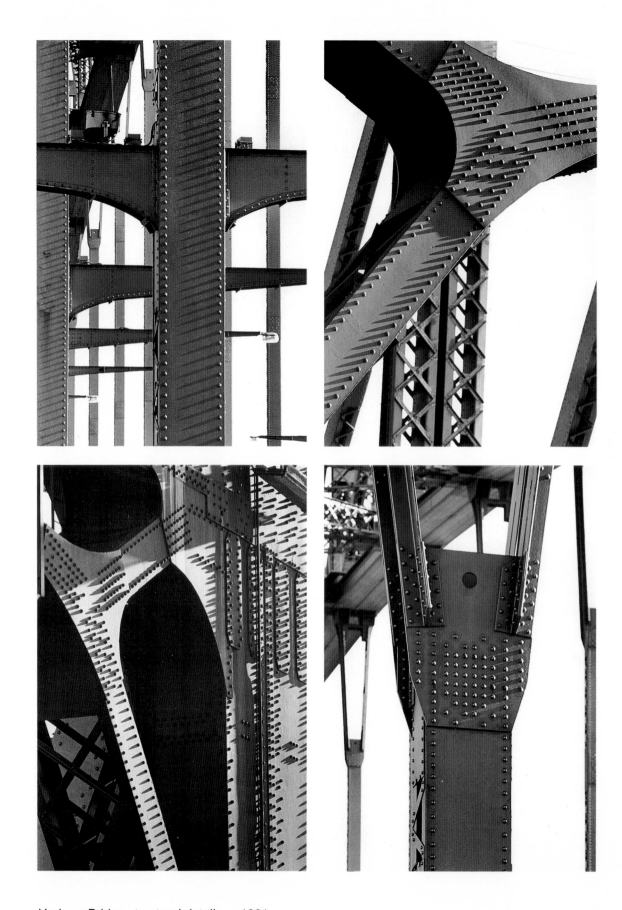

Harbour Bridge structural details – 1981

The bridge at night from Milsons Point – 1993

Western Distributor T structures, Darling Harbour – 1979

Western Distributor forms 2, Darling Harbour – 1979

THE OPERA HOUSE

Sir Eugene Goossens died in 1962, without setting foot inside the building he had dreamed of seeing built. The other visionary, architect Joern Utzon, fared little better. Despite the fact that funds for the project were largely raised by lottery, the cost to the taxpayer soared. In part this was said to have been due to massive quantities of building materials either vanishing from the site or in some way going missing before they were delivered, in part to the fact that as the structural problems were solved the solutions led to an unforeseen budget blow-out. Criticisms were constantly aired in public by a delighted press. The ongoing squabble about who would have the use of which hall in the finished building – the symphony orchestra or the opera company – broke out again and again.

It was characteristic of Australia at that time: the lottery, the inspired gamble of accepting a design which might not even stand up, the subsequent indifference to who used which theatre, and a depressing failure to grasp the importance of investing in the cultural enrichment of our lives anyway.

Accusations of scandal became a major issue in the State election and the government fell. The incoming government took over with self-righteous fervour. They stopped payment to the architect and Utzon felt driven to leave the country, unthanked and unnoticed – even his name removed from the noticeboard acknowledging the engineers and contractors. But, by the time he left, the skeleton of his great work was already a marvel of beauty.

He had solved the main structural challenges and solved them brilliantly. The rest had to be left to others: the interior spaces, the vast glass fronts, the cladding of the theatre walls, the stairway and the concourse. The architects engaged by the government made a very respectable job of it, in some cases an enlightened and sensitive job. But the strokes of inventive daring – the vision, the plans being exceeded by the actuality – these were gone.

Our legacy is an exterior, a fabulous freestanding sculpture loved by the very people who once mocked the concept as a waste of public money, enriching the lives of Sydneysiders as nothing else has, a building appearing as beautiful on a smoggy morning as it is by the full moon, or looming through veils of rain, or gleaming in sunlight, or crisply outlined against a deep blue sky.

Utzon is still alive and has never yet been adequately honoured by this country.

Sydney Opera House on completion of podium – 1962

Sydney Opera House construction 2 – 1965

Sydney Opera House construction – 1965

Sun patterns within the Opera House podium – 1962

Opera House west elevation, evening – 1966

Opera House dogman – 1967
Lifting roof section over Sydney Cove – 1967

Placing roof section, Sydney Opera House – 1965

Opera House riggers – 1966
Sealing roof joints – 1966

Opera House roof geometry – 1966

Architectural credit panel removed after resignation of Joern Utzon
Minister for Public Works the Hon. Davis Hughes – 1966

Opera House interior construction – 1967

Sunrise on the Opera House – 1966

Building the roof shells – 1966

Sun on the roof shells – 1983

Afternoon light on the Opera House – 1973

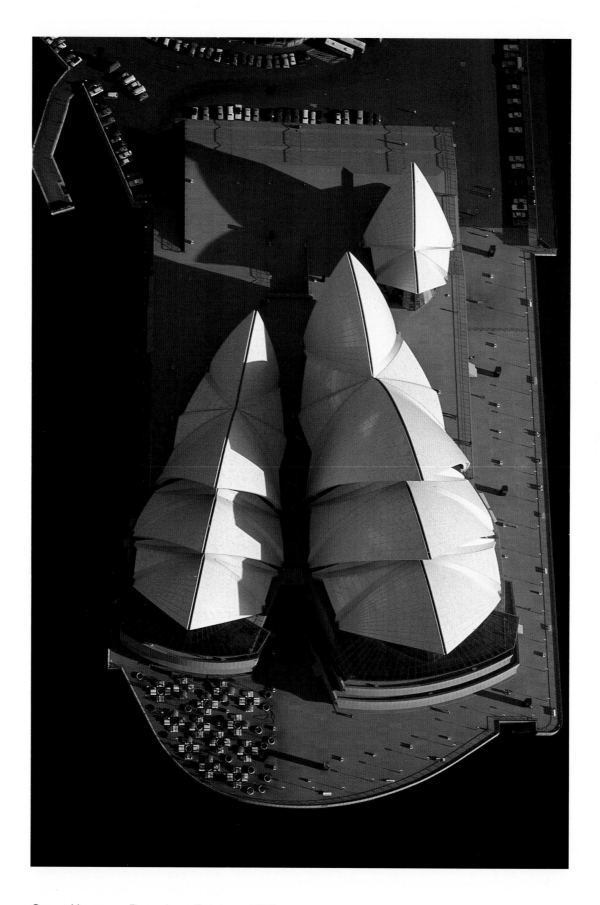

Opera House on Bennelong Point – c.1979

Sunrise on the roof shells – 1972

Migrant liner *Galileo Galilei* approaching Sydney Cove Passenger Terminal – 1966

Passengers on board *Galileo Galilei* – 1966

Girls on yacht, Store Beach – 1967

Sunday at Store Beach – 1967

Family in dinghy, Store Beach – 1967

Barbecue picnic at Store Beach – 1967

Sabot dinghies at Vaucluse – 1962

Gretel, Australia's first America's Cup challenger – 1962

Sabot dinghies and harbour lighthouse – 1962

18 footer with five man crew – 1962

Racing *Skip*, a 16 foot skiff – 1962

Start of sailboard marathon, Manly – 1984

Procession of Tall Ships, Australia Day – 1988

Bicentennial fireworks, Australia Day – 1988

Ship at sunset west of Harbour Bridge – 1985

Cyclist on Gladesville Bridge – c.1964

Summer dawn over Sydney from Kirribilli – 1993

Sunrise on the harbour from Cremorne Point – 1992

Sunset from MLC building – 1981

Dusk on the harbour from Watsons Bay – c.1965

Sydney Opera House with masts of *Bounty* – 1992

Australian National Maritime Museum and city at sunset – 1992

360 degree panorama of Sydney Harbour from martello tower at Fort Denison. Dawn through sunrise – 1992

Marine engineers' shed at Berrys Bay – 1992

▶

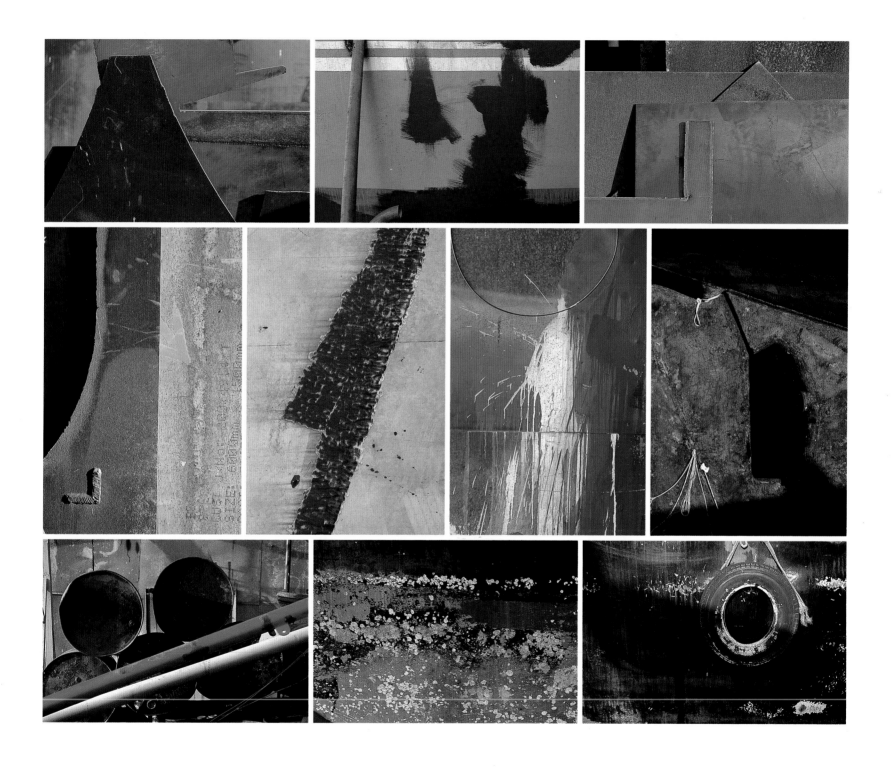

Shipyard details at Groom Bros. works – 1992

The city and Berrys Bay with Groom Bros. shipyard on foreshore – 1992

THE PEOPLE

In time the port functions dwindled: much of the freight was handled through other industrial harbours up and down the coast and passenger travel dropped sharply by the beginning of the 1970s so that the docking of great migrant ships was soon an event of the past. The airport became the point of entry for a new generation of arrivals.

Large sections of the harbour were transformed, wharves standing idle, moorings abandoned, piers empty and warehouses boarded up. Shipping was concentrated at the docks converted to container terminals, with the dehumanised scale of vast flat areas and widely spaced sheds. The fate of the docks not converted – which still stood abandoned and decaying – provided the subject for much speculation. From neglect as a result of lost functions they suddenly became the centre of interest. This was the first time in a century that waterfront districts right in the city had become available for large-scale civic planning.

Simultaneously there was an extraordinary coming together of intellectuals, trades unionists and the general public in support of preserving historic buildings, improving urban planning, providing parks and planting trees. 'Green bans' were put on threatened heritage sites and tremendous energy went into improving public awareness of the value of our past as well as the opportunities offered for our future.

Where the disused wharves were concerned, this was a matter of prime real estate. A lot of money could be involved. The issues were fiercely argued. The outcome was a civic plan to convert them to mainly recreational use. So Darling Harbour, in the heart of the old docklands, is now a site for museums, restaurants, exhibition spaces, and tourist shops. Circular Quay itself, having undergone a facelift, is far more inviting than it used to be, with pavement cafés and wide walkways for promenading. There is even a serious move in government to have the Cahill Expressway dismantled – removing that huge ugly blockage from across the face of the city so that Circular Quay may once more open out on a spacious plaza. Already the result of these changes has been to revive the waterfront as the heart of Sydney, a new Sydney – fashion conscious, wine drinking and theatre going – at one end connected to the heritage of restored terrace houses in Wolloomooloo and at the other to the heritage of restored pubs and warehouses in the Rocks.

There is an analogy here with the interest people have shown concerning the rediscovery of their family origins. Polish and Czech migrants whose parents Anglicised their names are reverting to the original spellings, Chinese families who have lived as Australians for a hundred and fifty years revive the traditional New Year celebrations, Greeks and Italians who had made their money and returned to their homelands come back to stay for good this time.

Life here is thoroughly metropolitan and yet by comparison with cities elsewhere the air is clean and the pressures are few. Tourism publicity based on selling Sydney as hedonistic comes close to the truth, cliché-ridden though it may be. This is a place given to pleasure, not just the strident pornography of Kings Cross or people flaunting their beautiful bodies in Oxford Street, but the gentler pleasures of good living and relaxation.

The harbour is once again the centre of town, as it was a century ago, and Sydneysiders revel in it. At weekends large numbers of visitors crowd the Rocks and Darling Harbour and take to the water in dinghies, yachts and motorboats. Picnickers sail across to delightful little coves inaccessible by road and wade ashore with their wine bottles and baskets of food.

The recreational aspect of the harbour, which had always been there of course, has now grown ostentatiously dominant. David Moore celebrates this in his compositions of massed sails, boating parties, sportsmen, bon vivants, and gleaming shorelines under vast luminous swaths of sky. He captures the inviting quality of the place, the accessibility, the beach culture as part of a sociable mixing and mingling. He achieves this effortlessly in the images he discovers because Sydney is his city and he understands it in all its rich nuances.

Just as the fifty year span between the first and last of these photographs shows the water traffic changing, and the uniform black of old cars giving way to the modern multicoloured glitter, the new city rising high above buildings of earlier generations, so it also shows changes in the people themselves: not only will a gang of labourers now include men of different national origins, but men whose expectations of life have changed too. The labourer with a carefully groomed beard (who can easily be imagined going out at night after work in an evening suit) is as new a phenomenon as the prefabricated concrete units of the bridge he helps to construct. Sydney has blossomed into a tolerant, pluralist city revelling in a combination of the sensuality of open air living coupled with the pleasures of sophisticated society.

People are proud of the range of cultural activities flourishing here, from orchestral concerts, nightclubs, museums and art galleries to the opera and many other theatres. Most importantly the plays being shown are often Australian, and Australian music is heard at concerts. There have even been Australian operas at the Opera House. The result is such tremendous growth in career opportunities for artists that the arts are at last escaping the shackles of imitating what is offered in Europe to take their place at the cutting edge of our imaginative enquiry into what kind of nation we are in that endless process of reshaping ourselves and our self-awareness.

The city responds with confidence.

Sydney is as much the people as the place. And the people are enthusiasts for fine food and wine. These are accepted pleasures, available to most sectors of society, as reflected in the massive array of fine eating houses offering cuisines from dozens of nationalities – besides our own versions developed to appeal to distinctively Australian tastes. The wines, likewise, include a magnificent range within reach of most pockets.

We have come a long way from the outpost, the tiny, fortified, convict-built port carved out of stillness at the remotest corner of the empire to provide British merchants with a base from which they could penetrate the valuable spice trade (which in its day was the equivalent of oil today as a source of immense wealth). And we have also come a long way from the sycophantic colony dutifully sending men and women off to fight in Britain's wars in New Zealand, South Africa, the Crimea, in France and Flanders and Singapore.

Not least of the changes is the impact of Aboriginal art on our iconography and our sense of identity. In this respect there is still an exciting future before us as we learn all we can from the first inhabitants of the land. A real start has been made and Aboriginal motifs, music and dance already occupy a powerful place in the collective consciousness.

There is real energy here. Small wonder that Sydney loves to let its hair down and celebrate, rising to just about any occasion with gusto, alive with people out for a good time. Nearly half a million cram the streets for the annual Gay and Lesbian Mardi Gras in March, revelling in the glittering ostentation and cheeky political abrasiveness. People feel good about belonging here. They are proud of the city, the lifestyle and the harbour.

Habitually, like winding rivers and creeks and the meandering back streets, we come again and again to the harbour. Driving past some dingy row of houses crowding in the shadow of a disused factory we may be suddenly confronted by a sheet of water dancing with sunlight or sleek and glamorous at night, a silky black mirror of a thousand lights. This affects the way the population thinks and behaves. To outsiders perhaps it is a brash place, perhaps it does flaunt its vulgarities. But for those who love it, this is part of the vitality, and essential to the beauty of the place, keeping its sophistication free of blandness.

After all, the space of such a harbour and its generous scale can support a good deal of garishness and get away with it.

Travelling to work by ferry or lounging at the waterfront on weekends we soak up the blue and golden light, soak up the moody tints of a cloudy evening with the water lying under a dull sheen, soak up wild windy days with the coves like sheets of deckled steel while trees toss along embankments and sails lean perilously flat to the water, we identify with the lone fisherman perched on his bollard replete with the dignity of a person contemplating the eternal verities. Of course – because we *are* that person.

The eye feasts on textures, as the camera does. We are drawn to gaze at ravishing patches of rust and oil, at odd blots of worn paint, at a used car tyre slung over the side of a boat for a fender and dangling there as round and unsurprisable as a fish's eye, at slapdash corrugated iron boatsheds, at weed-grown piles and decaying moorings. Drawn to them all the more after the photographer has educated us to value them.

A taste of the open sea is in the air. City buildings appear to crowd the water's edge. Trains rumble back and forth over the Harbour Bridge and a constant rush of cars converges on the bridge, crosses, and then unravels along a skein of roadways in the inner city: that brief passage over the water reaffirming the character of Sydney, reinforcing the special presence of the harbour. Even when drivers curse the bridge (which they regularly and habitually do, especially during the rush hour) they reaffirm its part in their lives.

The harbour is central to our notions of history: here the First Fleet arrived, just as here the Japanese mini-submarines sailed in on their mission to sink the US cruiser *Chicago*. This role in history was spectacularly underlined during the 1988 bicentenary celebrations. Beyond question the rest of Australia felt rather left out but Sydney didn't care. Sydney, with typical appetite for life, indulged itself in a riot of jubilant flags and lights, a thrilling parade of tall ships and a buoyant bobbing irrepressible multitude of merrymakers afloat in every conceivable kind of private craft and packed on shuttling ferries, while others swarmed along the wharves and through the lovely strips of parkland skirting the sandstone cliffs.

There is something in the spirit of the place, something greater than ourselves, and it affects generation after generation.

If anything, Sydney at a quiet time is even more breathtaking than the rowdy Sydney. In early morning when the waterway is as entirely empty as it ever gets, maybe a single ship or two dinghies out there, the whole vast surface can come alive with a million glitters, like nothing so much as a huge shuffling flock of silver birds – gone the moment the wind drops – leaving the dinghies becalmed above fathoms of blue water while, tucked away in a sheltered cove somebody's outboard motor coughs to life and a skiff slips off among moored yachts, pulling the thread of its wake through the silky surface, while along the nearest shore a lone jogger attends to his health (and we are brought up short by the realisation of how bizarre a jogger would have appeared to the Sydneysiders of 1943 ... or 1963 for that matter) and in the next bay a sun-tanned woman dives into her harbourside swimming pool at one of those luxurious houses with lawns winding down to a private jetty.

The mixture is unique: so much of the shore still wooded, the sculptured shelves of rock, the fresh clean city of clustered towers on either side, a combination of privileged villas for the rich, free pleasures for the poor (including nude bathing at Lady Jane Beach!) plus an immense extent of public waterfront complete with footpaths, benches and picnic tables. And just a few kilometres to the east the surf culture flourishes along fine sandy beaches where youths with bleached hair squat gazing out to sea assessing the swell, or skim inshore on their boards. The atmosphere is distinctive, particularly when a southerly buster blows in. As the poet Bruce Beaver puts it:

> Mid-day and a heat haze over all
> backed by the flue-black hammer of a storm.
> The ocean trundles barrels of waves
> up and down the shore ...

All things considered, a remarkable amount of the harbour foreshore still remains as wilderness, covered by relatively untouched scrub, ferns growing in the crevices, fairly much as it must have been since time immemorial, provided one doesn't look up at the towers of the city across the water. And to the north, a flat platform of sandstone lies concealed in the heath. This natural formation, so like a tessellated slab, worn level by aeons of exposure, is a kind of Bible inscribed on mottled rock. If you stare at it for long enough you can trace shallow carvings of fish and flocks of wallabies, men and women from another age, figures carrying boomerangs, and a hermaphrodite with legs splayed.

All round the visitor the virgin bush of the Ku-ring-gai Chase National Park spreads its vast carpet of subtle flowerings. There is not a building in sight or a sign of the city. Bees hum. How long, one wonders, did it take for news to reach this place that down at the water's edge things were changing? How long did the original inhabitants live on in this place before loss of their food supplies and their circuit of sacred places forced them to surrender or move away? How many were shot down? The wilderness reminds us of questions which many Australians still find uncomfortable but which must be faced before we can fully accept ourselves and take responsibility for our nation.

Surely it is no accident that the city grew without a centre, having no focal point after it ceased to be a port cupped around its dockland, being simply a place to work and something of a backstreet city with odd little laneways and a cramped layout quite unlike Melbourne's frontal presence and broad tree-lined boulevards. Sydney still has a kind of gritty inconvenience, a belated and inadequate stretching to meet the demands of choked traffic. The beaches and the harbour are its public face.

Cities the world over are accumulations of their own past – precious to those who live there for what they have been and what *we* have been – as much for what they are and what we are. Even with the devastation of much of the old city, Sydney's past is still clearly inscribed in this huddle and in such details as the little-used operator's box on a swing-bridge, empty warehouses and old navy stores, an obsolete power station (with cable-braced smokestacks) already brooding on the imminence of demolition, austere little churches and flamboyant department stores, boarded-up piers, channel lights in fancy housing with slatted skirts or miniature Georgian cupolas supported on hexagonal bases and slender columns, the Regency dazzle of the Hornby lighthouse on Inner South Head which was built in 1858 after the successive losses of the *Dunbar* and the *Catherine Adams*, Pinchgut (Fort Denison) commanding the centre of the waterway with its perfectly preserved martello tower, the peeling frivolities of Manly Wharf and Luna Park, the cast-iron balconies of the inner suburbs.

Photography is uniquely equipped to celebrate these things and to freeze them for us, each in its time frame, offering the delight of 'reading' the images for the kind of detail one would not have noticed at the time. Often such details evoke those special qualities which cannot be photographed: the air, the salt-fresh southerly that blows away tonnes of smog, the slap of waves along rocks, the creaking of ropes as a ferry ties up, the quiet click of bowls while white-clad players pad about in sponge-soled shoes occasionally offering a discreet patter of applause for somebody's fine stroke of judgement.

There are memories here of bygone work patterns, obsolete machinery, the carefree wildness of a kind of childhood no longer possible in the city. There are reminders of foggy mornings in rowing boats (how often is anyone seen rowing a boat these days unless to reach their yacht?) with a pea-souper drifting in to envelop the far shore where clustered steel cranes loom as shadowy presences, like portents of the imagination. Turning page after page of these photographs we watch the city manifest fleeting surprises and reminders of lost times.

The lasting impression is of a *used* city and a *used* harbour. Small lives of hardship and endurance interact with the large geometry of the bridge and modules for new structures being lifted aloft (although only the earlier pictures include those celebrated Sydney dogmen who once used to ride the load with daredevil ease). Images of the rich aboard expensive boats interact with the wasted resource of disused ferry wharves. In this evolution there is a cheerful mixing, perhaps tinged with irresponsibility, caught at benign moments on weekends when the magic of the water erupts with carnival life as the populace takes to boats and windsurfers.

Sydney may be seen as a city of inspired whims and mistakes. Just as the Opera House was a last minute rescue from discarded designs, so Captain Cook sailed past the heads and missed discovering the harbour itself, so the early Governors of New South Wales, who were naval officers to a man, failed to erect any warning system for their own ships approaching the heads and the task fell to the first Governor with no navy background, Lachlan Macquarie. This lighthouse, which is the last building you see as you leave by air, was designed by Francis Greenway and completed in 1816. The Governor and the convict architect stood side by side in the official party (in itself a strikingly Australian thing for them to do) and 'drank success to it in a glass of Cherry Brandy'.

Just as the element of chance should be acknowledged, so any celebration of what we have achieved in this wonderful place needs setting in the context of lost opportunities. These lost opportunities, too many to number, were mirrored for years by the lost talent of our brightest artists and scientists leaving to pursue permanent careers in England and America – inventors like Lawrence Hargrave whose experiments in aviation we neglected, only to find they were snapped up overseas and used by others. The richest resource we have brought here – ideas – has been constantly undervalued. Perhaps even this will change, given time.

When you fly out of Sydney, leaving the glitter of the city behind, you can see the coastline as a vast sandstone platform eaten away by waves. Down along this coast Hargrave flew his frail box-kites. And here, perched on top of the cliffs, stands the Macquarie Lighthouse. Shining a light out to sea may seem a curiously frail gesture in the context of such massive landforms confronting such a limitless force of pounding water. Yet the lighthouse and its warning light are a reminder of where so many Australians came from and the hazards of getting here. They are a reminder of this land as an island and as the most ancient and worn-down slab of the earth's crust.

Rising into the late afternoon sky, with that exhilarating lift of the wings bearing you up, you can still look back and see the harbour laid out as a gilded dragon on a silk scroll. Like an ancient work of art. Immediately beneath your aircraft a trawler may be returning, in from the vast crosshatched sea, with its cargo of fish for the markets. Twenty-four nautical miles off the heads the vessel will sail above a shelf, and here the skipper may see on his depth sounder, far below the keel, a lost shoreline from before the Ice Age. It will show up on his screen in primary-colour contours: the indentation of a drowned river mouth – as far below him as he is below the departing plane. This is the original river, flooded when Sydney Harbour was created.

Glebe Island Bridge construction site – 1992

Scott Wyatt, Mario Perkovic and Merv Francis working on Glebe Island Bridge – 1992

Construction of approach to Glebe Island Bridge – 1993

Riggers on Kingshaw support structure, Glebe Island Bridge – 1993

Sydney Harbour Tunnel construction worker – 1990

Construction of Sydney Harbour Tunnel, south side – 1990

Control cabin, Pyrmont Bridge – 1985

Pyrmont Bridge, Darling Harbour – 1985

Pyrmont docks with Naval Stores building – 1978

White Bay power station – 1978

Ship and wind patterns on western waterway – 1967

Tanker *Siratus* and western face of city from Greenwich – 1993

Cruise liner *Achille Lauro* berthing at Sydney Cove Passenger Terminal – dawn – 1991

Woolloomooloo finger wharf and Garden Island crane – 1990

Jogger and rising full moon with Garden Island Naval Base – 1991

Superstructure of HMAS *Melbourne* – 1985

Aircraft carrier HMAS *Melbourne* at Athol Bay – dusk – 1985

Evening yacht race and Oberon class submarine – 1991

Aircraft carrier USS *Independence* departing Sydney heads – 1992

Winter fog on the harbour – 1973

Harbour Bridge in fog – 1973

Kirribilli and the city with morning fog layer – 1991

Sunrise on the city from Vaucluse – 1992

Morning sun over Elizabeth Bay – 1991

The city at dusk from Mosman Bay – 1991

Campbells Cove and the city at dusk – 1992

Hornby lighthouse at South Head with rising full moon – 1991

Macquarie lighthouse and Pacific Ocean cliffs at dawn – 1993

Australian National Maritime Museum, Darling Harbour – 1992

Boys fishing under Pyrmont Bridge with afternoon light on the city – 1992

Boatshed at Balmain – 1978

Ladies' Day at Waverton Bowling Club – 1992

Sydney Harbour from 20,000 feet – 1992